THE ANALYST

THE ANALYST

POEMS

Molly Peacock

W. W. NORTON & COMPANY

Independent Publishers Since 1923

New York | London

For information about permission to reproduce selections from this book, write to Permissions, W. W. Norton & Company, Inc., 500 Fifth Avenue, New York, NY 10110

For information about special discounts for bulk purchases, please contact W. W. Norton Special Sales at specialsales@wwnorton.com or 800-233-4830

Manufacturing by LSC Communications
Book design by Chris Welch
Production manager: Lauren Abbate

ISBN: 978-0-393-25471-6

W. W. Norton & Company, Inc.
500 Fifth Avenue, New York, N.Y. 10110
www.wwnorton.com

W. W. Norton & Company Ltd.
15 Carlisle Street, London W1D 3BS

1 2 3 4 5 6 7 8 9 0

For Joan Stein

& Michael Groden

CONTENTS

PART TWO: The Hours

PART THREE: Ruby Roses, Kiss Goodbye

PART FOUR: Whisper of Liberty

ACKNOWLEDGMENTS

Grateful acknowledgment is made to the following journals, chapbook, and anthologies and to their editors in the United States, Canada, and the UK for publishing many of the poems in this book, often in earlier versions:

Alhambra Poetry Calendar: "Seeing Is a Meal in Itself" (under the title "Temptation") and "The Peephole"
Bellevue Review: "A Fall in the Fall" (under the title "The Fall")
Congeries: "The Analyst Draws"
Contemporary Verse 2: "Mandala in the Making," "Ruby Roses, Kiss Goodbye," and "Shadow"
Cortland Review: "Speaking of Painting and Bird Watching"
DMQ Review: "Authors"
Green Mountains Review: "Stirrups in the Emergency Room"
The Hudson Review: "The Carcass Coat" (under the title "The Carcass Coat's Journey"), "Dream Strawberry," and "In Our Unexpected Future"
Life and Legends: "Credo"

Literary Review of Canada: "The Analyst's Promise" (under the title "Promise")

Louisville Review: "Paid Love"

The Malahat Review: "Mount Anger"

The New Criterion: "George Herbert's Glasse of Blessings"

NewPoetry (Canada): "Contemplating Your Progress"

Partisan: "Tuesday Tombstone"

Plume (online and Annual): "A Face, a Cup," "Fret Not," "Gusto," "The Heaven of Lost Earrings" and "How to Say 'Thank You' in French"

Poetry: "The Nurse Tree"

Poetry London: "The Canning Jar" (under the title "The Jar")

Poetry Review: "The Massage"

Prairie Schooner: "The Analyst's Severe Arthritis," "Life, Lightened," and "The Pottery Jar"

Southwest Review: "Whisper of Liberty" (commissioned by Poets House for The Listening Room)

Taos Journal: "Pajama School" (under the title "Cut Outs")

Women's Voices for Change: "Hayfield Poetica"

The Yale Review: "The Analyst's Promise" (under the title "Promise")

Fifty Poems for Gordon Lightfoot (Brewery Bay Press): "Thoughts Are Things" (under the title "Song")

The Golden Shovel: Honoring the Legacy and Influence of Gwendolyn Brooks (University of Arkansas Press): "The Art of the Stroke"

A Ritual to Read Together: Poems in Conversation with William Stafford (Woodley Press): "The Analyst Draws"

A Turn Around the Mansion Grounds: Poems in Conversation & a Conversation (Slapering Hol Press): "Lucky Message"

The Word Exchange: Anglo-Saxon Poems in Translation (W. W. Norton & Company): "Riddle, or The Therapy Hour" and "Riddle: Moon and Sun"

The author thanks the Canada Council on the Arts for its generous support during the writing of these poems.

PART ONE

The Pottery Jar

GUSTO

Skin the asparagus for their lives,
whip the eggs, parmesan and chives,
miming your zest with my zeal . . .
Once, we shared a restaurant meal.
Slice the baby potatoes, skins on,
turn to the smooth black surface on
the stove where two steamers—enamel—
swim like red fish painted on enamel
and prepare with attention, like you,
my intimate witness, like you
who will never speak to me again
whom I will never see again,
hearing from your friend who tried
when you said, LET ME DIE,

I WANT TO DIE, to help you.
How horrible they got you
to the emergency room on time,
hemorrhaging in the brain,
a malformation that had lain in wait
seventy-seven years for you, supine,
slumped in your watercolor class.
Spoon the mustard and parsley sauce
on the perfectly steamed potatoes . . .
watching over them, keeping on my toes—

as you watched over me.
You were only forty
when you took me on.
Thirty-seven years! The stove is on.

The stove is a painting
from which the omelet leaps, and fainting,
folds in three on the plate
where sliced strawberry fins await.
And it was red food you ate with gusto at
the *ristorante* where we shared that goodbye meal
—I was off to grad school, done with therapy,
so we thought. Marinara sauce on the hint
of lipstick left on your lips, red on red.
Your dark brows swam across your forehead
as you watched me with a pure gaze,
and I watched back from the haze
of confusion—patient? or not.
Our new distance. The stove's still hot.

It was as if you'd painted my cranium
as a fishbowl: there my ideas swam.
Though my thoughts misfired for me,
you painted me a copy of their beauty.
With attention now, I eat my food all

alone, recalling the words of your friend
who brought your clothes to the hospital. Fraught.
"She can't say the names of her sons, though she can
still feed herself." Undone. But you eat,
the friend tells me, *with gusto*. "Hospital food?"
I say in shock. White on white. Humble,
the new appetite. *"No,"* your friend says,
"I sneak her lattes." Pain? *"Not in pain."*
White with a quick espresso stain.

THE ANALYST DRAWS

Two days after your stroke, they hold out the crayon
you vigorously reject. Four days on

without language,
you do what you loved before language:

pick up a pencil and draw.
"Do you *know* how much raw

rejection you take?" you asked me
one of the times we thought we'd ended therapy,

then said your Radcliffe professor taught
your studio class: ALL DRAWING IS THOUGHT.

But to you, abstraction was lying.
All you did was draw your father failing,

then dying. So when that man stalked to your easel
to deliver his raking critique, you walked

away from the studio—not to touch
a brush for thirty years. Brushes

you exchanged for words,
drawing from what you heard,

the lines of your patients' inner lives, teasing
out patterns for the easing

of the ~~raking~~, no, aching you saw.
So draw,

as I was drawn to you
as you drew me to you,

till I could walk away
as you now draw away.

THOUGHTS ARE THINGS

Thoughts are things—sometimes they are songs.
—H.D., TRIBUTE TO FREUD

How could you do it?
How could you do it?

I sing my little song.
I sing my little song.

What did I do?
What did I do?

She sings her little song.
She sings her little song.

You left me there.
You left me there.

I couldn't not do it.
I couldn't not do it.

That is your answer?
I cannot believe it.

That is my answer.
Again I have to ask her

Almost every day.
Almost every day.

GEORGE HERBERT'S GLASSE OF BLESSINGS

When God at first made man,
Having a glasse of blessings standing by; . . .
— "THE PULLEY," 1633

REST. George Herbert poured it last from the glasse.
People only find it at the bottom.
When I rolled down to the bottom
of the hotel bed, and the cell phone lit
with your number, I thought my torso had pressed it
—for you are in the rest of life now,
in the dregs of the blessings glasse.
In jet-lagged unrest I played the messages:
Your voice! With all the colors of its emotions
from cerulean to cerise. What were the colors
in the glasse of blessings? Herbert doesn't say.
Surely they were thalo and carmine? Instead he says,
"So strength first, then beautie flowed . . ."
but your words were garbled and weak. Slow.
Yet your message hemorrhaged its color into air

—in half-syllables after your brain hemorrhage.
I heard your voice as in a painting: CAN'T. BE. YOUR. PSYCHO-
THERAPIST. ANYMORE. Meta to physical. Brain to torso . . .
Think of a hand-blown goblet Herbert himself
might have held, bubbled and thick, yet pouring out
"the world's riches." So the cell phone hadn't spoken out
from a dream, but from the waking life—
where "wisdome, honour," flowed, from a life

partly wakened, restless with a ready urge to be,
and feel "pleasure," Herbert's second-to-last "treasure."
The last part was clear: CALL WHEN YOU GET HOME!
Then date and time in stately monotone.
It takes such strength to call, I can't search now
for why—though all our enterprise was for why.
The bottom of the glass is standing by,
                              the rest.

SPEAKING OF PAINTING AND
BIRD WATCHING

"Do you remember my friend Katie?"
I ask when you and I talk on the phone.
We skirt around the blast hole in your memory:
your stroke and aphasia left a singed edge.
As we talk around that burnt gorge—
a gouge of thirty-two years—you can recall
a thing or two about the distant past.
"Do you remember her, the artist?"

> (*"I never envy great artists,"*
> Katie whispered on her screened-in porch
> keeping quiet for the hummingbirds.
> *"It's the trendy ones who make* me *jealous.*
> *For artists who move me, I feel only love."*)

"Let me remind you: Katie's the one
whose boyfriend I fell in love with and almost
leapt into the gorge with, but didn't—"

> (*"Don't disturb possible hummingbirds!"*
> Katie whispered on the porch where,
> mournfully, we talked about other avians,
> the red-winged blackbirds of our childhood:

how we toddled out importantly
with bread crusts in our hands and tossed them to
the multitudes nervously flocking around.)

"—and the boyfriend became
a therapist, certainly not as good
as you were, before . . ."

(Last summer Katie saw no red-wing,
but I spied one on the way to her farmhouse
among her great old trees. *"I intend to die
in this house, but,"* she said, *"if something
happens to my trees, I'll have to move."*

That one red-wing I saw, was it as lonely
in its rarity as I assumed? Or not, as Katie said,
"It just knows the world it was born in.")

Yes, when you and I talk on the phone now,
I feel a thrilling red patch.
"They take me to the park every day,"
you tell me. "And they take me . . .
what's the word?"

The burnt edge of the memory gorge
you have to make a path around
starts to crumble—don't fall in!
"The place . . .

with the things on the walls . . ."
Blackness.
A museum?
"Yes! Museum." Red word.

"All I want to do is go away and paint
—just like I did as a girl."

> (When I told Katie the whole story
> of your aphasia, she whispered,
> *"That is like my trees dying*
> *and having to move . . ."*)

Unlike the red-wing, you know more
than the world you were reborn in:
"I can't be your therapist ever again,"
you repeat to me.
"I know."
I still can't help whispering,
"I thought I'd never hear your voice again."

("If someone chain-sawed my big trees,
Katie said, *"I could never paint the stumps*
like those fancy-asses who draw them
just for the design . . .")

Your low tone of realism sets in:
"I might never get back to Italy to paint.
But I'm working really hard."

(Then Katie and I heard
the low buzz of a hummingbird.)

FRET NOT

When you welcomed me for the first time since
your brain hemorrhaged, you looked so trim and well
in black and white you could almost convince
us both you were whole. Your living room welled
with light, the wall above the couch arranged
with your watercolors. "I hung them myself,"
you said proudly. Almost nothing was changed
(except for the attendant, making herself
small by sitting silently). You're witnessed now,
as you've witnessed me. "May I have a painting?"
I'd been afraid to ask, but I did somehow.
"You really want one of my paintings?
Then come in here." *Your bedroom?* But I was
your patient! Before your brain bled. Yes, *was.*

I followed you into the narrow room:
plain as plain. Like a nun's cell, the bed,
a single pallet, no headboard, a deep red
blanket instead of a coverlet. Blood bloom.
Nuns fret not at their convent's narrow room.
No one could climb into that cot but one.
A tall row of wooden cabinets. One
you opened, and small paintings that had loomed
above my head (as I'd lain on your couch
and talked about, around, for, yet, because . . . and wept)
you brought out now from where you slept.

Your pallet. Next to your palette.
Red blanket like a hemorrhage contained
after a time bomb exploded your brain.

The painting I chose was small: two lemons
against a blue background, one with a tip,
a salmon-colored aureola. Lemons
like breasts, nurturing companions, the tip
of a sensuous world on a piece of paper
folding out and beyond and inward and
onto the contours of the conquered land
of your mind, landmined. We're. *Were.*
You laid the yellow watercolor down
on your bed, a camp cot for the wounded
in a tent pitched on a plot of scanty ground.
Fret not. Fret you not. Forget-me-not: found.
So I lifted it up—then laid it in this frame
now on my wall. Hourly I pass your name.

THE POTTERY JAR

Thank you for asking me not to smoke,
thank you for the extra ten minutes no charge.
Thank you for knowing the smoke that seeped
beneath the heavy gray apartment door
was war poison from afar.
Thank you for your chic haircut—
every therapist should have one.
Thank you for not condescending to
that Navy man who had such bad
Depression-era karma he secured
the soles of his shoes with rubber bands
and the farm girl who leapt from reading books
behind the barn into her Book of Life.
Chapter Two: Post War,
in which the wounded Navy boy threw
his farm girl down the cellar stairs.

Thank you for your posture, bolt upright,
when I was so mad I declared I could break
the antique pottery jar on your shelf.

Chapter One: War.
It's always backwards in analysis, isn't it?
Thank you for reading my injured mother
who aided a game her child played—
wherein the little girl walked with a cane, bandaged
from head to toe in sheets torn up for kitchen rags.

Thank you for warning me on the phone
that now you'd be walking with a cane.

Thank you for not believing me when I said I was suicidal
(my dad had died and evaporated into smoke
—that rageful man, yes, slowly I admitted I had
half his genes—bomb-vaporous beneath
the heavy gray apartment door).

How could you take her seriously,
a young woman living alone from paycheck
to paycheck in a studio on the Upper East Side
rehearsing Sylvia Plath:
She opens the stove, crouches down on the floor
and stops before she rests her head on the oven door
to think, *How sticky this is!*
Thank you for waiting decades for her to acquire
a sense of humor as well as better clothes.

After I declared I'd break the gray jar
with navy blue patterns, after your posture,
bolt-upright in your chair—
you said, "You will *not!*"
(What if the farm girl on the cellar stairs
had shouted, YOU WILL NOT?)
When I reached for that dishtowel

to lay on the oven door, practicing my mini-death
in response to Daddy's falling, then positioned
my head on the checkered terry cloth,
I must have thought, *You will not.*

Thank you for addressing me as "honey."
Thank you for carrying me when I had no money.

Thank you for waving goodbye as that young woman
set off to cohabit with a man who wore a bathrobe
till 5 in the afternoon and smelled of Balkan Sobranies,
and thank you for the welcome back.
Thank you for your applause as she changed
the locks and the password to the bank account,
for now she had a bank account.

Thank you for filling
the pottery jar with mimosa.
Thank you for your patience as she
decided the moral act would be abortion.
Thank you for knowing I could never
have children and survive.
Thank you for all those years when my sister was alive,
for waiting in the wicker rocker as I lay on the couch
and came to the beachhead vision of my sister
down a great hole flirting and begging me

to hold her hand as I crawled, prone,
to the edge of the sand where the crevasse began
(*it was war, it was war, it was war*),
reaching down, knowing the edge would crumble.
Thank you for not calling her a sociopath.
Thank you for witnessing this use of the imagination:
I began to creep away from the crevasse,
it was war, away from the ocean of her heroin addiction,
the calls, the money, the methadone.
Thank you for poise and ease.
Thank you for simply standing
as I learned how to stand on the sand.

Thank you for repeating that now you'd be walking with a cane.

Thank you for those occasional cups of tea.
Thank you for the boundary, perimeter, thin
blue lines on a gray pottery jar,
drawn lines, fine lines, fine distinctions.
Thank you for your soigné, distingué look.
Thank you for watching as I achieved my distinction.

Thank you for taking the young woman's friend in despair,
vaporizing into smoke before her eyes.
Thank you for the artful schedule—they never passed in the hall.

Thank you for that silhouette I saw
wearing your earrings and belt
as I stood at a podium before a darkened theatre,
the vast audience unmoved after I failed to entertain.
Thank you for tolerating that woman's wild hope
of a genetic link to Thomas Love Peacock
whose satirical glee straightened her spine as she walked offstage
refusing the routine after-drinks.

How long does a girl have to wear a gas mask, anyway?

Thank you for repeating
"I know
I can't
always
speak the right words"
(for your stroke erased many words),
"But I want
you to know . . .
(Thanks again for warning me about the cane.)
. . . how much I
care about you,"
and thank you for forgetting you've said it.
For if one has to hear a sentence again and again,
let it not be *it was war, it was war, it was war,*

but those twenty-one words
as if poured in spurts
from an antique pottery jar
that sweats with cool joy
on a humid late summer day
in a room with a woman and her cane.

THE ART OF THE STROKE

Each body has its art, its precious prescribed
Pose

—GWENDOLYN BROOKS

Each body has its art. All parts of you, each
artery and vein of your brain, make a body,
and if part of it explodes, your soul still has
a place in the rest, doesn't it? Doesn't its
essence still speak, still practice its art
even when you can't fill a sentence with its
words? You still eat with gusto! That's a precious
urge from your hand to your tongue, desire prescribed.
Isn't there a special yoga pose

of Spoon-in-Hand? Your living will may oppose
the state you're in, but your specialist prescribed
acute rehab. All you claimed as precious
surfaced in a single sentence that forced its
meaning, LET ME DIE, to create an ending art
with the soul—that's what's left, isn't it?—as sculptor of its
ragged material. And when the soul has
finished the work of its clay heart, clay brain, clay body
each spark can misfire and each body part, each . . .

PART TWO

The Hours

LUCKY MESSAGE

The bottle's salty voyage took
three years from when those boys
tucked a note with your address
and *SEND THIS BACK TO US*,
then tossed it from the ship

into the sea. In the ecstasy
after their note was returned
by a sailor who took the bother,
one boy's father offered
a job to the other boy's father,

and your whole family moved
3,000 miles to the little town
where I had a job, too,
(just escaped from the smashed
glass of my father's bottles).

He'd been a sailor.
                    Do you
remember the slanted floors,
like a ship's deck, of the room
in the office you had there? You'd leapt
into your practice. Desperate

I was—*Tell me what to do!*—
gagged by the stench in the glass,
the trapped fumes, lost years
stoppered up, unbreathed.
Don't send me back there.

But you had to. Into
that old house by the water,
where we sat together
as I asked and I asked and you held,
came a destiny smell:

I'd thought that the tang
in my nostrils was the taste
of tears, but it was a brine,
something to float on, the salt
of the advice you never gave.

RIDDLE, OR THE THERAPY HOUR

A translation from the Anglo-Saxon Riddle 72 (K-D 74)

I was a girl,   a gray queen,
and a man, solo,   all in a single hour.
I flew with the birds   swam in the seas
dove under waves   died with the fishes
and stepped out on earth   —alive, all in a single soul.

Traditional answer to this riddle: SHIP'S FIGUREHEAD

CREDO

I believe in being killed, and I believe in poetry.
Let's begin with a word, you say. That word's not clear.

(I don't believe you when you say you'll help me.)
I believe in being killed, and I believe in poetry.

The mouth of the past contorts with uncried tears.
What would it even mean to help me?

At tea a lady says, "Career."
At home a fist lifts up a glass of beer.

I believe in poetry. I believe in a will to be.
Let's begin with a word, you say. And I say, "Fear."

MOUNT ANGER

It began as liquid
a mountain rush of fear
the breakage of hidden springs
into grief-tears then tiers
of earthwater gushing
but the flow thickened
—snotty bloody clotty
as the tissues heaped
industrial pyramids of
used Kleenex
—then the urge
just not to flow anymore.
To be solid—that
was good, wasn't it?
Firming up? But the false
solidity became mounds
of charred waste.
Up from this smelt
rose Anger,
bulbous-legged
ham-armed
its creaking abdominals
turning side to side.
Then I was in the arms of Slag.
We thundered toward all
that was clean,

people, paper
the newly vacuumed couch.
We brought the Big Dirt
into the subway
among the innocents,
Anger's hands huge
Anger's haunches huge.
We lumbered into restaurants
roaring, *Where's the manager?*
Why don't you water
those dying plants?
Are you running
a concentration camp
for flowers?

Our jaws could eat cement.
Anger chomped at
the marriage wall
ate the glass windows of friendship
and bled from its stone teeth,
muttering, *Oh not, I am not, at all, at all*
I am not at all,
then lay with its belly full
and answered the phone nicely.
Later it slid through
security lines

with my passport between
its teeth
so it would shut up and smile.

But like all things manufactured
Anger aimed to get smaller
I am not, not at all, at all
and dried itself hard
and grainy, yellow-tan,
small as cat food pellets,
far, far from the bloody fur
and guts of a rabbit
in a kitty mouth.
Uncrushed by my incisors,
horked down whole,
it traveled the length of
intestines that wrapped the globe
to come out in its pellet form
without arms or legs anymore,
no mouth
nothing but grief
still undigested
hard ersatz spoor.

THE CANNING JAR

In White House Meats at St. Lawrence Market
a rabbit lay in the case, next to the quail:
perfectly skinned, head still on, eyes still in,
its tongue hanging slightly out of its mouth,
small, pink. "Not with the head on," a woman
whispered in a lilting voice to a man.
Thump, thump. When my first marriage broke up,
I got a four-month rental, and a rabbit.
How lonely it must have been by itself
in my furnitureless place. I wasn't even thirty,
couldn't quite take care of myself or
the spotted rabbit who met me at the door,
peed on the white bedspread, left a pellet trail
across the rug, bit the refrigerator cord

completely through, and started a kitchen fire.
My sister brought her ragged hippy friends
and their little daughter to my happy
empty new apartment. The girl loved the bunny,
and I gave it to her, with the cage and food.
She held the rabbit close to her chest, its hind
quarters tucked in her hands, as I'd shown her.
Thump, thump. I packed up my place and left
for graduate school. Thanksgiving came and went.
The holidays. Then the cold spring. Up, up
I drove to the mountain shack my sister had.

The mother of the girl was there, clean-faced
in her ragged dress. "That rabbit is a guard dog!"
she said. "Thumps in its cage when someone comes."

So now the rabbit lived outdoors in its cage,
and thumped, and grew a woolly coat. "Warns us
better than a dog!" she marveled. The other
rabbits they had didn't do that. Oh, they had
others. They were much poorer than my sister,
who gave them extra food stamps for their girl.
"Two free-range boneless skinless chicken breasts,"
I said to Joe at the White House counter when
the whispering woman left. "She didn't
mention the rabbit," I said to my sister
the next winter when the clean-faced woman
left, in too-big boots, to walk through the snow
with her food stamps. Thump, thump. My naïveté
disgusted my sister.

                    "They ate it, Molly,"
she said dryly. That was always what they
intended to do. That was why she brought them
up to my place when I was packing to go
to graduate school. My sister was working hard
to unscrew a lid from her tomato jar.
She canned all her food herself. I saw her

do what our father did when he worked, hard
at something with pliers or a wrench.
He stuck his tongue between his teeth before
he gripped, and whatever it was sprang loose.
My sister put her tongue, pink, small, between
her lips, pulled, sprung loose the lid of her jar
and began her stew.

THE ANALYST'S PROMISE

When we see me slump, defeated in my chair,
should we disturb me? Or should we leave me there
in my cave, in my brain, my truck, lake, lair,

dive, booth, toilet seat, back bench, bar-
stool-equivalent of slumping in my chair
undressed, in my pajamas, unaware?

Though groomed, me looks tousled. Me's three:
something's frayed or delayed—and me's back there,
through wadis, through arroyos, where the glare

of an absorbing sun sucks the moist air into a wheeze.
Me breathes a shallow breath, defeated in my chair.
Snug hood of fear. I'll never shout or dare

to have a bold idea or simply stretch in ease
or find someone worth beguiling while I'm lost in there.
But that's my fear to conquer. Till I repair,

I must not leap. Not call, cajole, mock, or appease
when I slouch, defeated, even in a straight-back or
a dentist's chair, desk chair, club chair, a theatre seat.

Don't we all deserve a good slump, even so deep
it unnerves the loving witness? Me will not please
her. She is the goddess constructed of the air

methinks I need to breathe, but don't need.
Agreed. We'll leave me there.

HOW TO SAY "THANK YOU" IN FRENCH

http://www.wikihow.com/Say-Thank-You-in-French

Method 1: Basic Thanks

1

Say "merci." This is the standard, most basic way of saying "thank you" or "thanks" in French.

Merci for seeing me.
To be seen, important thing in life, most.

2

Add "madame" or "monsieur" after it. If you want your *merci* to sound a little more formal, you could address the other person as "madame" or "monsieur" after expressing your gratitude.

Merci, madame for not raising your eyebrows at *mon monsieur, spécialement* when I declare,
"I think I'm going to get married again."

Method 2: Adding Emphasis

1

Use "merci beaucoup." This phrase means "thank you very much" or "many thanks."

Merci beaucoup for asking to meet him.
Merci beaucoup for saying, "I've always liked men with his looks."
Merci beaucoup for your silence as I hysterically mention that *mon fiancé* has just passed the five-year cancer recurrence mark.

Silence.

2

Switch to "merci bien." This is another expression used to say "thank you very much." *Bien* is usually used to mean "well" or "good," but it can also mean "very" . . . *bien* is being used to express emphasis on the strong nature of the thanks.

Merci bien for twenty-one years of taking his side as I railed against his habits: setting the alarm, all timed to his shockingly limited point of view. (Everything isn't always logic you know!)

Merci bien for *vingt et un* years of quietly standing beside a sliver of a shadow of his *logique* while never saying I am *une névrosée. Hysterique.* Usually about *rien.*

3

Express extreme gratitude with "mille fois merci." This expression roughly translates into "a thousand times thanks" or "thanks a thousand times."

Mille fois merci for your voice: a rich, calm sea. As if a person heard the sea from lying on the beach in a painting by Matisse: *Luxe, calme et volupté.*

Là, tout n'est qu'ordre et beauté, Baudelaire *a écrit.* There, all is order and beauty. Henri *et* Charles were right, YOU were right. Why get *nerveux* about it all? How about a little more *volupté,* or *calme,* at least?

To be heard, important thing in life, most.

Method 3: Full Sentence Format

1

Tell someone familiar "Je te remercie." This translates to "I thank you." . . . *Te* is a second person pronoun used to indicate that you are speaking to someone you are familiar with. It can be used with friends and family.

Je te remercie for your painterly point of view.
Did you always have to paint me a picture?
Yes, to learn anything, I had to see it.

It was as if I gave you all the elements and you reassembled them into a 45-minute painting—who am I kidding? I mean 90 minutes since I never got anything done in a single session.

Je te remercie, je te remercie for the *petite* capacity inside me for stepping outside myself. Yes! *C'est possible!* How little my mother could step outside. But she tried valiantly. What a deep love had we. *Ma mère limitée. Je te remercie* for the sea, *la mer,* in your voice.

2

Switch to "C'est vraiment gentil de ta part." This expression
means, "It is really kind of you."

    C'est vraiment gentil de ta part to be really kind to
me. To remember, since I was born into violence, that your
kindness guides me to be kind.

    C'est vraiment gentil de ta part to remind me that, yes,
each of us is many-roomed.

    In my mansion, in a drawer in a cabinet upstairs in
a locked room lies a painted ivory miniature, its perspective
from the bottom of a flight of stairs. My sister, *ma sœur,* and
I look from the last step up to the top, into the face of:

    Le Monstre!

    Le Monstre Papa,
    face red from *alcool,*
    pushes a woman down the stairwell.
    Our *maman.*

    Others have guest rooms, not intruder *chambres.*
From others I have learned kindness. And French. *C'est
vraiment gentil de leur part.* It's very kind of them. Kindness is
wealth. And words. It was very kind of you, *mon analyste.*

3

Tell someone you do not know well "Je vous remercie." This is
a more formal, less familiar way to say, "I thank you." ... *Vous* is a
more polite way to address someone in the second person "you," so
this phrase is generally used with strangers and elders. For further
emphasis, you could also say "Je vous remercie de tout cœur,"
meaning, "I thank you from the bottom of my heart."

Now that you have become stranger and elder after
your terrible stroke, I use *vous*. Formal, no?

You speak a strange language, mixing up pronouns
and sending your doorman's neck snapping back to look at
us when you address him as SHE.

Je vous remercie de tout cœur for being alive. To have
you return from the dead allows me to thank you from the
bottom of my heart, which long ago I attempted to freeze in
imitation of *ma mère*, who froze her heart against *le monstre*.

But my attempt freeze-dried my heart instead!
When *ma sœur*, whom he violated,
came in desperation with a knife to hack my heart out,
it had dried into bits.
You and I have pieced the flinty fragments together.
Je vous remercie, je vous remercie de tout cœur.

4

Express formal written thanks with "Je vous adresse mes plus vifs remerciements." This expression is often included in formal letters and means, "I send you my most sincere thanks" or "I send you my warmest thanks."

Now that you repeat the same words over and over, I cannot talk too regularly on the telephone with you. For something sears into me after we have the same conversation *encore et encore*. I hang up the phone and sit listless in the country where I voyaged to marry my logical individual, still very much alive.

But I express my formal thanks, *plus vifs*, in cards, pictures of the sea, which you will never cross again. For after several years of saying, "If I could only get to Europe again," you changed the words, "I know I won't get there anymore."

Are you sad? *Triste?*

"A little," *un petit peu*, "but I am at peace with it."

Une paix personnelle. How *volupté*, to imagine you checking the bank of metal mailboxes in your New York City building, there finding a square envelope of *luxe* paper sent from Toronto. Inside: a picture of *la mer*, where all is order and beauty!

Open *la carte* to these words:

Je vous adresse mes plus vifs remerciements.

For my second chance, *merci*.
Later you will call and repeat, "How lucky I am."
J'ai de la chance, you say.
And I say, *J'ai de la chance,* back to you.

THE ANALYST'S SEVERE ARTHRITIS

Even when you had all your faculties
there were physical frailties.

Then you were harrowed
yet capable of attention.

Once I attended to you
as your eyes narrowed—

foreign, as if they'd lodged
in an animal's skull

and not below your pert forehead
intelligently inclined.

"Are you in pain?"
Your simple *yes*

displayed the degree.
Then a question flowered

as if from a painting of a skull:
"How did you know?"

"I saw it in your eyes."
How could you attend to me

while seized so?
Yet you insisted on going on,

so I positioned my head
and then my feet on your couch.

My resistance, your insistence,
grew twin stems

toward the desert flower
we painted together,

unable to leave
our harrowed hour.

TUESDAY TOMBSTONE

Please don't move that blank
square of a gravestone
off the calendar. Leave
our vacant appointment

as it is. That simple space
is just the shape of a tablet
I feel my way toward
as a child in a graveyard

moves toward the face
of a ruined monument
pocked and slanted,
its letters half-erased,

puts both arms around it
and pulls to help lift it—
a standing appointment
trying to stand.

PAID LOVE

"But you paid her, didn't you?"
Certainly, I say. (Isn't love free?)
"But you *paid* her to listen for . . ."
One thousand two-hundred and ninety-four hours.
Say you were in an accident, say you
had to begin a series of procedures . . .
Some years you might feel fixed—
walking and running and swimming
—but if a part of you,
your femur or ulna, your pelvis,
your seventh facial nerve,
started to weaken or fray,
you'd have to go back to that office again
endure the surgery, then perform

the hours of post-op exercises.
And partly healed injuries have
their own torque . . . Bones
(minds have bones) grow even
after they're operated on . . .
human growth as complicated
as every light-year to Aldebaran,
every hair on every bonobo,
every pistil of every aquilegia . . .
The analyst and I only understood
a minim of it all, a jot. Together

this became our joint art: my job
to feel my strength—to stretch and hurl
—hers to listen, question, watch things heal.

"But you paid her, didn't you?"
How that question endures.
Yes, because we live in an economy.
Because it didn't start out as love, but watching . . .
one's sightings in the telescope
the other's findings from the microscope
both with a fascinated reverence
for how we're made. Somewhere,
our meshed process became love.
"But it was *paid* love, wasn't it?"
Where else in life is the necessity for payment so clear?
You could call it making a living,
though now that it's over,
perhaps it's the pure unpaid love you mean.

PART THREE

Ruby Roses, Kiss Goodbye

RUBY ROSES, KISS GOODBYE

You, who saved me from hardening,
let me not harden now

but walk into the world, disarmed
yet escorted by these emissaries:

two ruby rose earrings, in echo
of years ago, when I passed my hand,

arm brushing my ear as I sobbed,
back to you, behind me in your chair

with your notes, glasses and clock.
You took my hand and brushed

my hair over my temple.
After each hour I always bought

some little thing. Today those earrings
—two ruby rose hard things

remind me not to harden.
Let me feel naked without them.

THE HEAVEN OF LOST EARRINGS

Go down the grate after the green
agate scarab with the frowny face,
then through the damp and the dark
—the heaven of lost earrings is not
a bright place. Curl with the crumbs
in the corner of a pocket in
the discarded clothing bin,
then climb up the unzipped flap
of a suitcase and meet me
next to the severed pearl.
In the velvet dark of reattachment,
through beach sand and grime
in lintballs, dustballs, dirtballs soft
as the earlobes they were lost from,
next to the carved blue lapis orb—

through the crack in the floor, beneath
the taxi seat, in the accordion seam
of a subway train, in the airplane toilet
on another plane altogether where a low
moan replaces the harp and keens,
"There must be two, there must be two,"
hurtling toward the midnight of reunions
where everyone forgets what started
their arguments, why one unclasped

so suddenly, or the other's stud just
dropped without a sound to bury itself
in a carpet in a lobby, and the loop
that contained the red droplet
with its cloisonné leaf sprang
down the cleft in an elevator shaft
after it, almost like Orpheus calling
for Eurydice, meet me.

                    The heaven
of lost earrings is not a hell, though
it's dark *down* there that becomes *up* here
on the other side of the world where
memories surface, carrying their own light
unlike the heaven of the airy risen.
This is a heaven of the fallen
where each fleck, each gold whorl,
each silver hinge gleams up in the murk
for its partner, searching through the rubble,
sniffing for the buttony smell of the other
till they click and clasp their clasps
or slide long wires into their studs at last
and glow not as on a stage or even in the light
of a windowsill, but as in the warmth
of an unmade bed just left by the gods

up hungry for their nectar, now
nestling alone, forgotten but for a stab
in the nerve-end lightning of a memory flash.
Meet me down there in the fold.

DREAM STRAWBERRY

after Marianne Moore

You've seen a strawberry that's had a struggle,
pucker-faced, summoning up its strength.
It can't seem to relax its vigilance.
A tiny red fist strains.

"These are heavenly strawberries!"
Pauline plucked one from the countertop,
then Edward sauntered in, eyes on the berries,
ate one from the bowl, and agreed.

At the real kitchen counter in my house,
(in a bowl once belonging to those now dead)
a plump, red seed-pocked struggler sits.

Its name? Nevertheless. In the dream,
bright as rain, those two reunited
—what I never understood, overcome.

HAYFIELD POETICA

1. Pauline's Poem

Pauline looked out at the timothy hay
and said to her daughter,
"If I wrote a poem . . ."

Molly looked up
and prompted her mother,
"If you wrote a poem . . ."

"It would be about the timothy."

Late August breeze:
screen door wheezing,
curtains moving on their own.

"THE TIMOTHY CHASES ITSELF TO THE FENCE."

That's all?
Now Pauline looked surprised.
Why would anyone need more?

Outside, the ripe
wind-rushed timothy leapt
into the arms of the fence,

caressed by the fence,
stopped by the fence.
"That's my poem," she said.

"One line."

2. Molly's Poem

"THE RUSHING, THE RUSTLING, THE HEAT.
THE GREEN, THE SILVER, THE FENCE.
THE WHIRLING FROM ROOTS AND THE BEAT
OF THE STALKY LEGS IN THEIR TRANCE."

The hay was almost like a flock
of cranes taking off, except
the timothy's legs were forever
anchored in unseen soil

like Pauline, a woman tethered
to the place she was born,
viewing through curtains
the field of long grain,

—same since she was young,
rushing to meet her date,
the crackle of static in her brush
as she sweeps her hair out to its limit.

AUTHORS

(1956)

1.

CHILD'S COLLAGE ILLUSTRATION: *The heads of Louisa May Alcott, Nathaniel Hawthorne, Herman Melville, Walt Whitman, and Ralph Waldo Emerson, cut out from an old deck of Authors cards, pasted between the crenellations at the top of a child's hand-drawn castle.*

Dowdy Louisa May Alcott could not
match her mirror card, now lost. Nathaniel
Hawthorne's mustache got crayoned, then torn off.
In the tiny girl-sized deck of Authors
ruins began small: a corner rip, then
sunlight started through (unlike full-fledged ruins,
grass-encroached castles where adults can turn
their ankles). Grimy, sticky, feminine
index fingers, not crossbows, destroyed
the twelve bearded card-men's faces and
Louisa May. Authors was what a mother
in exasperation told a girl to play.
After the deck's matching halves got lost
—only one Herman, one Walt, or Ralph Waldo—she
tossed a fresh deck in the toy box.

2.

CHILD'S COLLAGE ILLUSTRATION: *An arm tattooed
with a Nazi concentration camp number, cut from a* Life
magazine *photograph, pasted as if reaching down to a
Christmas tree, cut from the cover of* Woman's Day, *with
a hand-drawn tiny castle taped on as a top ornament.*

I searched the lines of Alcott's eyes for clues
to the gift I should buy—everyone
in our grade was to wrap a present for
the Christmas Grab Box. Yet everyone was
Jewish, except for two Catholic girls,
and Protestant me. Had Mrs. Calendar
forgotten the numbers on some mothers' arms?
When my mother took me to the store
to pick out something for fifty cents,
we browsed like tourists through a ruined castle,
looking down each aisle as into a moat:
Stuffed animals were at least a dollar—
twice the limit set. The toy store windows
cast shadows as late sun filtered through snow.

3.

CHILD'S COLLAGE ILLUSTRATION: *The top of a castle cut from* National Geographic *is mounted on a heavy piece of cardboard, painted black. Perfume bottles snipped from* Ladies' Home Journals *and gardenias from* Burpee's Seed *catalogs alternate between the crenellations. Slots cut into the bottom of the castle wall hold a Benjamin Franklin half dollar, a mercury dime, and two buffalo nickels, taped so they won't fall out.*

Motes of light struck hanging cardboards with toys
stapled to them. Something amber glowed:
a bottle of girls' perfume in the shape
of a miniature glass lamp. The label said,
GARDENIA. Seventy cents. "You could buy
Authors for fifty," my mother said. "*That*
won't be easy to wrap," said the toy man,
his hat and coat on. Time to go.
When my mother bought the perfume
with her grocery money, a stain spread—
a trickle-leak cracking a castle wall.

At home I pried the bottle from the cardboard,
opening the glass top, sniffing—TOILET it said
on the bottom in itty-bitty letters.

4.

CHILD'S COLLAGE ILLUSTRATION: *Nathaniel
Hawthorne's head, cut from an Authors card, is
superimposed on a WWII soldier in uniform dancing with
a woman wearing a corsage, cut out from* Look *magazine.*

"Before the War, when *I* was dating,
a man bought you a gardenia for your coat."
"What's toilet water?" "French for perfume."
Trying to tape the bottle back to the card,
I ruined the card, then just wrapped the bottle
with buttresses of candy cane paper.

At the Christmas Grab Bag various
fifty-cent gifts were drawn: a ball-and-jacks,
pick-up sticks, a piggy penny bank with
one cent shaking in it. Someone got a
crummy ten-pack of gum. I spied my perfume.
Should I grab my own gift? A tall girl from
the back of the room (we sat by height)
reached in and unwrapped it, disgruntled:

5.

CHILD'S COLLAGE ILLUSTRATION: *The figures of Jane and Sally running, cut from a used* Fun with Dick and Jane *reader, lead a parade of cut-outs from the* Buffalo Courier-Express *(a perfume bottle, a locket and a piggy bank) pasted into the top of a cardboard dress box from* The Sample Shop. *A metal jack, a single black plastic pick-up stick and a* Beeman's *gum wrapper are taped below them.*

"My mother won't let me wear perfume."
"THAT was over fifty cents," Mrs. Calendar
exclaimed. I was waiting too long, the gifts
diminishing. My hand jumped in and fished
out a small rectangle. A box for a locket?
Something jewel-like for sure. So neatly wrapped
—a mother had done that. Hard to break the tape.

Sometimes a ruin is just a foundation
of stones where a castle stood, stray fruit trees
clues to where a fortress was. It was sleeting
when my mother came to pick me up.
The heat smell rose in the wool upholstery
of our Dodge. "How was the Grab Bag?" *Fine.*
"What did you get?" *Authors.* "Oh well, you like Authors."

6.

CHILD'S COLLAGE ILLUSTRATION: *A photograph of a 1956 Dodge cut from* Popular Mechanics; *hand-drawn droplets of sleet in black crayon cut and pasted around the car.*

Tears feel so hot on a cold face—these
like the slush flying from the windshield.
"It's only a school grab bag," my mother said.
"The real Christmas is coming up!" Like cutting
brick after brick from page after page
to make a castle from old magazines
was how it felt to say what I felt.
                                        Home.
When my mother came upstairs to get me,
I wept volubly, inconsolably,
feverishly as when she died. The tiny
amber glass lampshade . . . it wasn't only
the disappointment, but that *someone else*
got it, and didn't love it, and that
I had to be satisfied with Authors . . .

7.

CHILD'S COLLAGE ILLUSTRATION: *Louisa May Alcott's*
face cut from a discarded Author's pack pasted as the head
on the figure of a housewife cut from Good Housekeeping
standing next to black-and-white photograph of a Red
Cross ambulance cut from The Buffalo Evening News.

Abandoning the dinner fixings,
my mother gunned the gas like Gertrude Stein
driving an ambulance through German lines
to the wounded French (Gertrude wasn't in the deck),
in sleeted danger back to the toy store where
she bought me TWO gardenia lamp perfumes.
They weren't as good as the first one, my own
gift in the rubble of the bag. I would
have torn the Authors deck in two if I'd
been able to grip the squat rectangle
of cards that withstood both my hands because
all those authors stood together in the game
she kept me playing, overseen by bottles
of possibility and outrage on the shelf above.

STIRRUPS IN THE EMERGENCY ROOM

The power goes out. A fog comes in.
We're trying to identify a pain
that sharpens and fades. A blunt knife, a pin?

stuck between the clitoris and its hood?
The power is out. A gray fog is in.
The number of sexual partners you have?

Just one, for eighteen years. *You atrophy
as you age,* she tells me. Pain is a trophy
that sharpens and fades. A blunt knife, a pin!

Can you rate this pain one to ten?
Moon-faced young intern. And me. Our sin?
Her power is out. My gray fog is in.

Fear-infused sympathy. *If I could,
I'd help you. I really really would.*
It fades to a four, then sharpens to ten.

We're talking micro-physiology here.
Urethra or clitoris? A paper cut!
Like a paper cut in my clit, my dear.

If I could construct her face from a piece
of paper I'd scissor a slash of a mouth
a nose gash, and angle two brows—No peace

in the night. I took half a Valium!
Her wince draws the *ology* from *gyn*.
My power goes out. Her gray fog rolls in.

She looks and finds nothing as I
found nothing visible or my husband
or our magnifying mirror. —I'd cut each eye

in that construction paper as two jagged holes
for a power vision that's out. The fog is in.
Pain sharpens and twists to a rotating pin.

She leaves me in a windowless room for an hour
(you can abstain from sex, but not from pain)
—and returns without a test result or referral

or even a topical cream. Do not scream.
*If you find the right gynecologist perhaps
a clitoral biopsy?* All answers end in a dream

of cancer. The fog that rolled in stays in,
like age. It only goes forward. Its power
just that—though memory's pin sharpens
and fades. *Take aspirin.* Oh, I do. It's gone in an hour.

PAJAMA SCHOOL

Scissoring past the paper dolls to cut
diamonds in her pajamas—a work of art!

—the child made a pattern passed down from yore,
from her Saxon family on a distant shore.

When a little more convalescent, she filled
a fountain pen and pushed it across full

sentences—homework on ruled lines.
Mr. Bradley said it was just an old exercise

when she returned to lessons. He let her paper descend
from his long translucent hand toward the garbage can.

Her mother threw out the pajamas.
The child was not hurt. She knew from her distant land

of convalescence that her mother and teacher
could not really see as she saw, who still carried the land

of illness inside, a cut-out place, all thought illuminated
like skin showing through diamonds cut in flannel.

Convalescence was an eyelet covering:
inside it, she learned more every day.

RIDDLE: MOON & SUN

Translated from the Anglo-Saxon Riddle 27 (K-D 29)

I watched a wonder,   a bright marauder,
bearing its booty   between its horns.
An etched ship of air,   a silver sky-sliver,
it lugged a month's loot   from its raid on time
to build a great bower   from all it brought back
—if only it might   make plunder into art.

Climbing the sky-cliffs   rose another wonder
its dazzle known   to all dwellers on earth.
It seized the spoils   and drove the silver creature
with all its wrecked wishes   off to the west
(hurling back insults   as it hurried home).
Dust rose to heaven.   Dew fell on earth.
Night went forth.   Nothing afterwards then.
No man knew how   to map its path.

PART FOUR

Whisper of Liberty

LIFE, LIGHTENED

Like a runaway artist, you used to flee
your patients' modern anguish at home

to stroll along the ochre squares of Rome,
to sketch a yellow leaf, a tawny hound,

to see unvarnished color with free eyes
far from our jaundiced complaints,

from having to be wise—as you've escaped
from all of us now, your therapy room

now a *studiolo*, with a gallery of work
you'd never have hung before,

for fear of disturbing "our work."
And after your attendant

guides you up the elevator that
we, your patients, rode (almost over-

weighting it with our emotions
so some days it barely chugged

to the tan walls of the 21st floor)
you approach your door with

yellow mimosa that you'll paint, after
you unlock it, having learned

to use keys again, holding
both hands to twist the cylinder.

When you lived as an artist on the lam
for that month each year, you used

the watercolor pencils in your hand
not to note our dreams

(and now, who cares?)
but to draw the jonquil things you saw,

and live the raw *I am*, as you do now,
relearning how to show

the few of us who stay in touch
how to twist and learn.

A FACE, A CUP

The thousand hairline cracks in an aged face
match the hairline cracks in an aged cup
and come from similar insults: careless, base
self-absorbed gestures from a younger face,
cruel and fine. Bang! Each disturbed trace
deepens to a visible crack. A break-up,
a mix-up, a wild mistake: these show in a face
like the hairline cracks in an ancient cup.

Neither wholly broken nor all used up
the cup becomes a visage, unstable.
One never knows what will crack it open
and finish it. Banged too hard on a table?
Yet happiness might crack a face open
in a better way: hairline tracery as laugh lines
releasing the joys of ancient thoughts
cupped into use, and suddenly able.

SHADOW

A shadow behind me not my shadow
for it clings exactly to my back's back,
curls with me in the bed, alights with me
as I get up, crawls completely over
my shoulder to watch the meadow of things
I've laid for breakfast drift across the table.
It is sleepy, not heavy, just with me.
Yet I forget it—or should I say . . . you?
—and for hours feel nothing at my back
while sunlight casts the dwellings' long shadows
into the busy city streets cut over
and under by traffic, a mist of things
I purposefully stride through. But not you.
You cause the wobble of my ankle
before I regain my poise at the curb,
asleep on my back in the noise, undisturbed.

THE CARCASS COAT

Stitch, stitch, and sing, I hum my lonely song
while sewing skins of what apart was torn.
And soon I'll drag a coat of pelts along,
small things, once bright-eyed, trapped then worn.

I sew to reattach them, hide by hide . . .
But when my coat skims the floor in full view,
a bestial vestige, others give me a wide
path in the airport corridor—in lieu

of looking at me, they look at *it*:
a crusted coat, with stiffened hair of fear.
Why is that gray-coiffed woman, chic and fit,
carrying a . . . a *carcass* behind her? No one leers,

openly at least. (They quickly look behind
to see what *they've* been dragging.) *It's bright decades,*
I say to them calmly, head inclined
in the candor of beseeching, *trapped decades.*

My seatmate asks, "How much does that thing weigh?"
I try to whisper, *It won't get in your way,*
but blurt, *I've lost my way,* instead. Alarmed,
the stranger helps me shove it in the overhead.

THE MASSAGE

Lying on the table feeling the spine
Relax (nothing to do) a tear forms,
Just one—could it be the same each time?
The tiny insults of the day, forlorn,
Now clarified so a tear can form
And slide down the cliff of the cheek each time,
Melting into a padded plain. There, the spine,
Under the shadow of another, forms
Its fresh idea: one can't do this alone.

CONTEMPLATING YOUR PROGRESS

Thomas Crawford's sculpture, 1856
Stroke due to arteriovenus malformation, 2012

The New-York Historical Society.
Huge white marble sculpture in the lobby:
Dying Indian Chief Contemplating

the Progress of Western Civilization.
You duck beneath him with your wobbly cane
then upturn your face toward his, contemplating

his sober view of hysterical society.
"Something terrible has happened!" you say loudly
as a teenage girl to the sculpted dying man.

"He's so sad!" you repeat to the empty lobby
where we make a pair, a society of two
(plus a volunteer and a guard) contemplating

the mystery of the new you, brain torqued
from your stroke. You connect without history
—but with feelings whole—to the agony

of the Dying Indian Chief in marble.
Your fresh response remakes his catastrophe.
Yes, something terrible has happened—

we amble on. "That's a very sad man back there."
Progress comes. With a cane. Without piety.
Wake up a statue. Then repair.

SEEING IS A MEAL IN ITSELF

At the Doyle auction galleries, New York

When I think, *I wish you could see this*, you
leap out and double my shadow with your own.
Winter sun at our back, our shadow zips
us across the street against the light, then
steps us through the auction gallery door.

How we love the porcelain lamps
of Lena Horne's estate—her *chinoiserie!*
There are her caftans, her jewelry.
What small shoulders she had, you whisper
up from our interior. Noon. Time to take off—

past the Noritake plates, lacquered trays
and hand-painted table. We flee through
the glass door triumphantly buying nothing,
and you fall back asleep beneath my skin.
I hardly notice your flickering pulse

as I order lunch in a coffee shop
lifting a small-shouldered oval bowl
of coleslaw, to cherish its thickness
scratched, inhabited, like a long absence
turned into nourishment.

THE NURSE TREE

Why waste away in a box
when you could be a nurse tree?
That's what they call dead logs:
mushroomeries of the woods.

Your living room's a wood
of couches, books, and chairs.
You're dead not at all, but
could you be preparing

for things to grow inside
the chest of the log
you plan to become:
cherished compost heap

where heat turns the brown
mess of feelings, sorry,
that's *peelings*, into comp-o-
sition? For we who love

our hands in dirt, a leaf skirt
*de*composing seems an ideal
station between this life and
next: I visit your room

as on a forest walk. Passing
a fallen log—is that you?—
I see a scarlet fungus cap
pop up from friable bark.

A FALL IN THE FALL

Thus I; faltering forward,
Leaves around me falling,
Wind oozing thin through the thorn from norward,
And the woman calling.

—THOMAS HARDY, "THE VOICE"

Lesson 1: Drop

My husband rises up like the face of the cliff
of helpless love, the stone of exasperation,
the slip of frustration. "Don't
overdramatize," he cautions feebly,
as he drops me at the desk
of my analyst's building.
Crossing the lobby, slippery
black stone steps loom up,
a long wet staircase, cut into a cliff.
I hold the elevator open
with my cane and ease in
—up to the 21st floor.

Vigorous, she comes to the door.
My, aren't you moving well!
Smart haircut.
Me? Fallen tree with a drooping head.
I drop into a chair she motions toward: *her* chair,
where I have never sat before.

Did I really do it? Fall on purpose—as *she* fell?
Did I grab the stone instead of the railing
to feel the rock rush at me?
To refuse to descend gracefully?
Therefore to stumble. And fall accidentally.

"I'm so old," she says. Eighty!
She can just read the dedication,
on the birthday present I've brought.
With the Turkish rug between us:
She sits on the *couch*. In *my* old place.
I in *hers*.
Where have we ~~fallen~~ landed?

With sublime practicality we order up,
and our egg salad sandwiches rise 21 storeys
along with two lidded cups of hot chocolate.
A lunch I adored as a child.
"Good!" she says,
and banishes her helper to the bedroom,
so we are *tête-à-tête*.
"How did it happen?" she demands, in charge.
I am small. Weak. Still.
She enlarged, moving.

Lesson 2: Lucky

Less than a minute after "This is danger—"
(not even the *ous* could fly from my mouth),
I'd pitched forward in the dark.

My fall itself fell,
rising up, both cliff and pit,
as my ankles slammed
the angles of the stairs
and my shoulder smashed
against a fist of rock.

"I am lucky."
That's what *she* always says about her health.
I did not die.
I am not paralyzed from the neck down or in a body cast.
I did not bleed from the brain, as she did.

"Are you all right? Are you all right?"
people asked me, collapsed at an inhuman angle
amidst wet fallen leaves. *Don't touch me yet,*
I whispered. *Let me see if I can move.*
Call my husband.

Some part of my branch snapped, my analyst said
when the stroke changed her life in thirty seconds—
she had fallen from the great height of her height,
five hundred feet, was it? No,
about five feet three inches, collapsing
in an inhuman angle on the floor.

Some branches broken off become
walking sticks.
Where is her cane?
There, stowed in a corner.
She's asking about my life,
as she used to, when she had a practice,
a place where adults, *the experienced*,
could be small and still.

Why be ashamed of falling down a staircase
to arrive and be mothered by my former analyst?

Lesson 3: Watch

We want those we love to stand unaided.
"What were you thinking?" my husband persists.
"Just hurrying, as people do," I say lamely,
now that I am lame. My feet are blue—
all the internal bleeding drained down
to my toes. "Next time," he declares,
"you have to insist that people watch out for you."

It's only in the autumn that we really watch trees.
Leaves just hurrying down, as they do.
How happy children are to play in heaps of them.
How happy I was just to eat an egg salad sandwich
as if I had come home from school.

Time for acetaminophen and ibuprofen.
Time to change my ankle wraps.
Time for my sling.

Let's live in the unconscious.
Let's live in the imagination.
Let's live in the practical world together, too.

Inside the word Fall flourishes: *ALL.*

When we go out, I forget my cane
and have to limp back to get it.
Lessons. Don't they have to be absorbed?

Lesson 4: Joking Around

"When I signed up for IN-SICKNESS-AND-IN-HEALTH
twenty-two years ago," my husband declares, chuckling as he
untangles the cord from the unwieldy hairdryer,
"I didn't think it meant hairdressing!"

(I will not be able to lift my arm for six weeks,
and he will have to style my bob.)
The whole mess strikes us both as funny.
My analyst's (excuse me, former analyst's)
birthday is over, life resuming.

Of course we married each other to parent each other.
Our poor parents tried, but they slipped
and tossed us both up in the air.
The minute we left their hands we began
grasping for one another even though
we hadn't even seen a speck of each other in the distance yet.

My sense of humor circles like an eagle.
My husband's sense of humor circles like another eagle
beyond the river's cliff.
Eagles don't soar only to chase.
Over the fall trees on the river, they soar to play.
My husband's hand hovers with the hairdryer,
and the strands of my hair
fall into some sort of place.

THE PEEPHOLE

Please come to our stub
at the end of a branch
                              off
a branch of the family tree.
You can hardly see us
through all the begats:
the leaves of generations
of babies from ladies
and ladies from babies
and men and men and men.

None of us are dressed
in skins or silks or uniforms.
We are all just names
written on our leaves—
Here is our stub!
Can you see it among
their densities, the leaf cities
of begats from continents
and ages overlapping
in green upon green?

Something ends
with two leaves on a twig,
life not always for
getting.
   Here,
when all are there,
the sky shows through
a peephole: a leaf hole
shapes
getting nowhere
out of the blue.

WHISPER OF LIBERTY

A line curls
from voice to ear.
Haze on a harbor sings
then clears.

An insect wing
makes a creepy satin
swish on skin,
and you hear it.

A line curls
between love
and anything but:
a slap on a map

as a border shuts.
Miniaturely military,
a tiny cavalry
yanks on one end

so the line recoils
before it recalls
its other end can
curl to a wing.

Its wish?
Not to knot
as a necktie but be
a lace for a shoe running past.

IN OUR UNEXPECTED FUTURE

paintings of Anders Zorn at the National Academy Museum

Love-sadness prances across the flounces
of peach-gowned women in old-fashioned portraits
as an anniversary presses us toward them.
(*Stick-stick*: the sound of your cane tip on marble.)
All their agitated longings and fears
pulse through ruched necklines, palpate
in taffeta waistlines, outliving their societies,
pillars and palaces burnt in a blink.

The painter berobed their dreads in clothing,
uncomfortable ruffles of hopes that billow below
such careful faces, their moody moods hiding
in folds of silk, surviving silk—

for frocks outlast pillars. But feelings
outlive frocks. The immaterial storms through,
a force beyond years (a mere four since you
were nearly felled). It isn't what happened that lasts.
Not art, either, but the savory core. What's felt.
We relish your reprieve as if we'd licked all
the way through the paint, leaving wet marks
to vanish from gowns long gone (but not).

MANDALA IN THE MAKING

at the Asia Society

Three Tibetan monks make a sand painting
(under spotlights) in a reverential hush,
the circular world before them everything:

a cosmos, a brain, a divine palace lush
with lotuses and pagodas in children's
paintbox colors. "Excuse me, my friend is

recovering from an accident. She's a . . .
painter. May we ask you some questions?"
(Have I introduced *you*, my former analyst,

as my painter-*friend*?) You point with your cane
to the mandala-in-sand and ask, "*Three*
artists? How do they decide who does what?"

"He's the boss!" One monk points to the other.
The boss beams above the bowls and brass funnel
he wields like a wand. When they're done,

they'll brush it all away. You can't believe it.
Nothing stays (including the memory you've lost).
What lasts? The pattern the monks have

memorized. Their burnt-down temple re-
turns as this circular core.

Only when
something's over can its shape materialize.

NOTES

Joan Workman Stein (b. October 17, 1934, Providence, Rhode Island) originally studied to become a visual artist, but at Radcliffe College instead became a psychology major. After graduation in 1956, marriage and the birth of two sons, she received her MSW from the University of Washington and became a counselor at Binghamton University. She then pursued her psychoanalytic training at the Postgraduate Center for Mental Health (now the Postgraduate Psychoanalytic Society & Institute) in New York City. Stein practiced in New York from 1980 until 2012 when a stroke caused her to close her practice. She now lives and paints in Seattle, Washington.

"The Art of the Stroke" is a "Golden Shovel," a poem based on Gwendolyn Brooks' sonnet, "Still do I keep my look, my identity . . ." The words of Brooks' opening, "Each body has its art, its precious prescribed / Pose," become the end words of each line in the first stanza of "The Art of the Stroke." This sequence of words reverses in the second stanza.

WITH THANKS:

To Phillis Levin, first of all, for her attention to the drafts of these poems, and, as always, to my husband, Michael Groden. Thanks as well to David and Jonathan Stein, Barbara Blum, Carole Munter, and Dale Singer for their insight and support. My gratitude goes to the editors of the journals, both online and print, in the United States, Canada, and the UK who have been the champions of these poems. Their encouragement urged me on with the many experiments that became *The Analyst*. I am also grateful to my agents Ellen Levine and Alexa Stark at Trident Media, as well as to my editor Jill Bialosky for her poet's eye and sensibility, to assistant editor Maria Rogers, and to Dan Wells, publisher at Biblioasis, for his faith in this work. *The Analyst* owes its final polish to the Norton design team. Lastly, I wish to thank The Brewster Inn on Cazenovia Lake for its calm hospitality.

Molly Peacock is a widely anthologized poet whose work is included in leading literary journals in the United States, Canada, and the UK, as well as in *The Best of the Best American Poetry* and *The Oxford Book of American Poetry*. She is the author of six previous volumes of poems, including *The Second Blush* and *Cornucopia: New and Selected Poems*. She has been instrumental in bringing poetry to large audiences through her instigation of the Poetry in Motion program on New York City's buses and subways and through her creation of the *Best Canadian Poetry in English* series. As a prose writer, she is the author of *The Paper Garden: Mrs. Delany Begins Her Life's Work at 72*, a biography of eighteenth-century collage artist Mary Delany; *Paradise, Piece by Piece*, a memoir about her choice not to have children; and *Alphabetique: 26 Characteristic Fictions*, tiny tales with illustrations by Kara Kosaka. Her poetry is the subject of a monograph by Jason Guriel, *Molly Peacock: A Critical Introduction*. She is based in Toronto and New York.